Given in honor of
William Penn Tucker

TRACY MEMORIAL
NEW LONDON, N.H.

WELCOME

The door is open wide—
The beacon burning bright-Ah, look!
Man's greatest gift to man inside—
A Book

by
William A. Obenshain

A History of American Music

FOLK

Christopher Handyside

Heinemann Library
Chicago, Illinois

Photo research by Hannah Taylor, Maria Joannou,
and Erica Newbery
Designed by Philippa Baile and Ron Kamen
Printed in China by WKT Company Limited

10 09 08 07 06
10 9 8 7 6 5 4 3 2 1

Library of Congress Cataloging-in-Publication Data
Handyside, Chris.
Folk / Christopher Handyside.
p. cm. – (A history of American music)
Includes bibliographical references (p.   ) and
index.
ISBN 1-4034-8150-4 (hc)
1. Folk music–United States–History and criticism–
Juvenile literature.
I. Title. II. Series.
ML3551.H25 2006
781.62'13'009–dc22   2005019282

Acknowledgments
The author and publishers are grateful to the
following for permission to reproduce copyright
material:
Corbis pp. 39 (Daniel Laine), 34 (Flip Schulke), 34,
37 (Henry Diltz), 19, 39 (Neal Preston), 43 bottom
(Vaughn Youtz); Corbis/Bettmann pp. 13, 21, 27, 31;
Getty Images pp. 26 (Alfred Eisenstaedt), 33, 38
(Bernard Gotfryd), 32 (Blank Archives); Getty
Images/Hulton Archive pp. 9, 8, 30 (Frank Driggs
Collection), 12, 22 (Stringer), 24-25, 28; Getty
Images/Time Life Pictures pp. 7, 18, 28, 29; John
Byrne Cooke Photos p. 29; Lebrecht Images p. 14;
Library of Congress pp. 5, 11, 15, 16-17; Magnum
Images p. 25 (Burt Glinn); Topham/AP p. 40;
Topham Picturepoint pp. 20, 42; Redferns/Gems p.
35; Redferns/Michael Ochs Archive pp. 36, 41; Rex
Features pp. 36, 43 top.

Cover photograph of a folk musician reproduced
with permission of Redferns (Michael Ochs
Archive).

The publishers would like to thank Patrick Allen for
his assistance in the preparation of this book.

Every effort has been made to contact copyright
holders of any material reproduced in this book.
Any omissions will be rectified in subsequent
printings if notice is given to the publishers.

Words shown in **boldface** are defined in the
glossary on page 46.

Contents

What is Folk Music?

In simple terms, "folk music" is the music that is created and played by people within communities, and passed down through generations. Every country and ethnic group in the world has its own popular form of folk music.

The United States is a country made up of immigrants. When people settled in the United States, or were brought here as slaves, they brought their music with them. Over the years, they passed that music down from generation to generation. In its early years, folk music developed as a regional form of music. Many of the first folk songs were **ballads**. Ballads are songs that tell stories of remarkable people, places, and events that have become legends.

A good example of the ballad is the early American folk legend of John Henry. As the story goes, John Henry was an African American who could hammer holes into rocks along the rail track faster than any machine. He once raced a modern machine and won. However, he died immediately after the race from the effort (with a huge hammer in his hand). Though John Henry's tale is told from the perspective of an African American, the ballad form is derived from folk music brought to the United States by English, Irish, and Scottish immigrants. Black musicians borrowed the form from their rural neighbors.

The adoption of other musical cultures is common in folk music. More importantly, thousands of old folk songs like "John Henry" survive as part of an **oral tradition**. An oral tradition is one in which the stories of a culture—and their ceremonial, religious, or dance music—is passed to neighbors and family members and between generations. Each new person takes up the form and adds their own specific details to make it their own. Folk music is a crucial part of oral tradition.

In the United States, the term "folk music" can also mean other forms of American music—blues and country music, as well as some rock, jazz, and R&B. But folk music, no matter what it's called, is about continuing an oral tradition that is many hundreds of years old.

For the purposes of this book, folk music is the music performed by rural musicians that spreads naturally through informal gatherings of people. In the late 1800s, **folklorists** began studying the folk music in America. They were trying to document the music that African slaves had brought over, as well as the music from the British Isles (Ireland, Scotland, Wales, and England).

A country fiddler, photographed in the late 1800s.

As early as 1867, folklorists published *Slave Songs of the United States,* sheet music that documented the songs of slavery. Not long after, *The English and Scottish Popular Ballads* were making the rounds in American universities.

These songs found their way from the rural populations of farmers and laborers in places like Appalachia and the Mississippi Delta. This music had taken root years before recording technology became widely available in the 1920s.

Little things would make a big difference. For example, in the late 1800s, a troupe of Swiss singers toured the southern states. They introduced **yodeling** to country folk. Folk singers and "old-time" country artists took a liking to yodeling and incorporated it as a singing technique in their own music.

By the 1920s, folklorists from universities and amateur **anthropologists** began to search rural southern areas to try to record some of the songs sung by country people. This is how folk music became known outside the rural areas where it was created. As the industrial boom took off, folk blues found an audience in the big cities of the North.

Folk blues was the form of blues played by rural blacks in the early 1900s. The music that is now referred to as "country" was first documented in 1917. In the first half of the 1900s, folk music continued to develop as a voice of protest and storytelling, largely by rural white musicians and singers. In the 1960s, it merged with rock 'n' roll and evolved quickly into a **multi-faceted** genre.

Thomas Edison invented the phonograph in 1877. This photo of Edison with his invention was taken in 1888.

Ralph Peer's Discoveries

The commercial beginnings of folk music happened almost by accident. In the early 1900s, Ralph Peer drove around the South searching for undiscovered talent for Victor Records in New York City. He had already recorded the first black blues song, Mamie Smith's "Crazy Blues," in 1920. In Atlanta, in 1923, Peer stumbled upon a local mill worker named Fiddlin' John Carson. Peer recorded Carson's "The Little Old Log Cabin in the Lane." This was, arguably, the first country music recording.

Then, in August of 1927, Peer struck good fortune when the Carter Family (A.P., Sara, and Maybelle) knocked on his door. In a makeshift studio in a deserted factory in Bristol, Tennessee, Peer captured on tape two of the most important sets of recordings in American folk music history. These recordings would eventually kick-start the country music industry. The group recorded a handful of songs that had been handed down through their family for generations. Songs like "Bury Me Under the Weeping Willow," "The Storms Are on the Ocean," and "Will the Circle Be Unbroken" became the building blocks of folk and country music. Of particular interest was guitarist Maybelle's unique form of playing. Maybelle would pick the melody on the lower strings of her guitar while simultaneously strumming the rhythm on the higher strings. This was known as the "Carter Style." The **acoustic** guitar was a key instrument in folk music. Maybelle Carter's style would have a tremendous influence on future folk and country guitar playing.

Maybelle (left), A.P., and Sara Carter in 1937.

Jimmie Rodgers had worked as a brakeman on the railroads. He became known as "The Singing Brakeman."

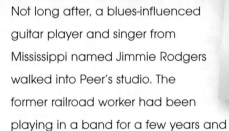

Not long after, a blues-influenced guitar player and singer from Mississippi named Jimmie Rodgers walked into Peer's studio. The former railroad worker had been playing in a band for a few years and had come with them to perform for Peer. But the band got into an argument, so Rodgers tried out solo. His solo audition was good enough to land him a chance to record for Victor Records. His first blues-based record, featuring his distinctive yodeling technique, was called "Blue Yodel." It sold more than a million copies and led to a run of national hits. Many people consider Rodgers to be the first star of country music. Sadly, he died of tuberculosis in 1933, at the age of 36.

The influence of the Carter Family, Jimmie Rodgers, and other ballad-based rural musicians had a big effect on the commercial development of country music. The straightforward, powerful way their songs were performed also made a deep impact on the folk music artists of the 1930s and 1940s. Two artists that were particularly influenced by the Carters and Rodgers were the Massachusetts' banjo player Pete Seeger and an Oklahoma songwriter named Woodie Guthrie.

Leadbelly

One of the major influences on the folk music that would become popular in the 1940s was a man named Huddie Ledbetter—or just "Leadbelly" for short. Born in Mooringsport, Louisiana in 1885, Leadbelly helped keep folk blues alive by recording hundreds of songs. He became a popular figure in the New York City folk scene and would even perform in Europe before his death in 1949.

Leadbelly's career did not get off to a good start. He had learned to play the guitar by the time he was 12, and by age 20 he hit the road to become a performing musician. But Leadbelly soon got into a lot of trouble for various crimes and spent ten of the next 20 years in different prisons. While he was behind bars, blues music was rapidly changing, and jazz was becoming the most popular music in the United States. His isolation, and the isolation of the other prisoners from whom he learned many of his songs, certainly kept modern influences from affecting his music. In this sense, Leadbelly was like a jukebox from a past time.

In 1930, Leadbelly was sent to Louisiana's Angola Prison. While he was there, folklorists John and Alan Lomax visited Angola to record the songs of prisoners. Leadbelly was one of the men they recorded, first in 1933 and then again in 1934.

Leadbelly introduced many of the songs that would become standards of both folk and folk blues, such as "Goodnight, Irene" and "The Midnight Special." These songs had been taught to Leadbelly by his relatives, friends, fellow prisoners, and other musicians. Some of his songs dated back to the time of the Civil War. This made Leadbelly a crucial link in the chain of folk music.

One of Leadbelly's prisons was
a work camp, and Leadbelly
led the prison work songs.

After Leadbelly's release from prison in 1934, he became John Lomax's chauffeur and recording assistant. He was also Lomax's guide on extended trips throughout the South, collecting songs performed by prisoners. On a trip to an Arkansas prison they recorded a prisoner singing "Rock Island Line." This became one of Leadbelly's more popular songs when he performed live. Lomax also took Leadbelly back to the Northeast, where he performed for college audiences and became a media sensation. Lomax managed to get Leadbelly a deal with the ARC record label that recorded 40 of his more bluesy songs. However, by the end of 1935, Lomax and Leadbelly had parted company.

Leadbelly eventually found a place in New York City's growing folk music community. This group of artists included Woodie Guthrie, Pete Seeger, and Sonny Terry and Brownie McGee. They were very active in using their music to express their political beliefs, which included labor rights, civil rights, and anti-war protest. Leadbelly and his music fit into the civil rights part of the struggle. After he moved to the city, he performed frequently to interested audiences. Leadbelly also recorded many more songs for the Library of Congress between 1937 and 1939.

This photo of Leadbelly performing at an informal gathering was taken in 1940.

Alan Lomax performing in the American School of the Air *radio show in 1939.*

The Lomax influence

The emergence of folk music as a cultural influence blossomed during the **Great Depression**. Under President Franklin Delano Roosevelt's "New Deal," the **Works Progress Administration (WPA)** was started. Some parts of the WPA program helped jobless people find work building dams, highways, and other major construction projects.

Another beneficiary of the WPA was the Library of Congress. The Library commissioned and sponsored John Lomax, and later his son Alan Lomax, to travel throughout the South documenting the folk music of America. They also traveled to the tip of Maine and to the Caribbean. Until about 1941, when the country started its preparations for World War II, thousands of recordings were logged for the Library.

Alan Lomax set about making sure that the music didn't sit in the Library and collect dust. He organized concerts in New York City for many of the artists he'd recorded over the years. These concerts drew a great deal of media interest, which helped spread folk music all over the United States.

In 1940, Leadbelly became a radio star on the many folk music related shows broadcast from New York City. He even hosted his own show, Folksongs of America. Leadbelly continued on a non-stop series of recordings that were released on many different labels, even after his death. Leadbelly was on tour in Europe in 1949 when he was diagnosed with ALS, or Lou Gehrig's disease. The illness progressed quickly and by December 1949, Leadbelly was dead.

Even after his death, Leadbelly's music lived on. Pete Seeger's group, the Weavers, recorded a popular version of "Goodnight, Irene." "The Midnight Special" was a hit not just once, but three times. The Tiny Grimes Quintet (1948), Johnny Rivers (1960), and Creedence Clearwater Revival (1967) all recorded their own versions. An early English rock 'n' roller named Lonnie Donegan **covered** Leadbelly's song "Rock Island Line." Among Donegan's biggest fans were the four teenagers who later formed the Beatles. It is impossible to overestimate Leadbelly's role in bringing folk's oral tradition to a new generation. His influence is still being felt more than five decades after his death.

Woodie Guthrie

Woodie Guthrie
in 1936.

In 1912, Woodrow Wilson (Woodie) Guthrie was born in Okemah, Oklahoma. By the time he was in his late teens, Guthrie was hopping on freight cars and traveling across the country. The oil boom that had supported the local economy dried up by 1931, and Guthrie went to Texas looking for adventure and work. Along the way, he occupied himself with writing songs and drawing pictures. In 1935, soil erosion and drought turned Oklahoma into part of what became known as "the **Dust Bowl**."

While he was traveling around the country, Guthrie was struck by the vastness and beauty of the American landscape. He also noticed the boundaries that were going up, keeping ordinary citizens from wandering freely in the country. The result of this **epiphany** was Guthrie's masterpiece and most famous song, "This Land Is Your Land," written in 1940. The song described a vast United States full of wide-open spaces and natural treasures where its people could roam free. It also criticized landowners and others who tried to put up fences and prevent American citizens from truly enjoying their country.

This land is your land, this land is my land.
From California, to the New York Island,
From the redwood forest, to the gulf-stream waters,
This land was made for you and me.

As I was walkin' I saw a sign there,
And that sign said "no tresspassin,"
But on the other side .... it didn't say nothin,
Now that side was made for you and me!

(This Land Is Your Land Woodie Guthrie)

This photo, taken in 1935, shows the devastation in Oklahoma caused by the dust storms that year.

Guthrie witnessed the terrible results of constant dust storms. Oklahoma residents were forced to trek cross-country to California, in order to flee the devastation in their home state. Guthrie joined this western journey. John Steinbeck later wrote about this mass exodus in his novel, *The Grapes of Wrath*. The Oklahomans' tragedy affected Guthrie so much that he wrote a song based on one of Steinbeck's characters called "Tom Joad." Later, Guthrie fan Bruce Springsteen would be inspired by both Guthrie and Steinbeck in creating his Grammy-winning album of folk songs, *The Ghost of Tom Joad*.

Guthrie spent the late 1930s in Los Angeles, trying to make it as one-half of a country duo with Maxine Crissman, or "Lefty Lou" as she was known. It was there that he developed songs that would become his first set of recordings. These songs documented his travels and his memories of Oklahoma. Guthrie next headed to the Pacific Northwest to find work. He found inspiration and employment working on the building of the Grand Coulee Dam in the state of Washington. The project was part of President Roosevelt's WPA. Guthrie was so moved by what he saw that he penned the song "Grand Coulee Dam" in 1942.

This photo of the Grand Coulee Dam under construction was taken in 1940.

Guthrie was first recorded by Alan Lomax in March 1940. He sang several of his original songs, including "Talking Dust Bowl Blues." Unlike many folk singers who took older songs and changed them slightly to reflect their own style, Guthrie's songs were often totally original compositions. From the time he started singing and performing in the late 1930s, until his illness made it no longer possible, Guthrie would write new songs or lyrics nearly every day of his life.

Guthrie moved to New York City in 1941. At this time, the city was a hub of cultural and political **activism**. Many of the folk singers in town were protesting the United States' involvement in World War II. These **pacifists** were much more concerned about improving the conditions for factory and farm workers in the United States than fighting a war abroad. Some of the folk singers were affiliated with the Communist Party, one of the groups which helped organize labor unions to defend the rights of workers.

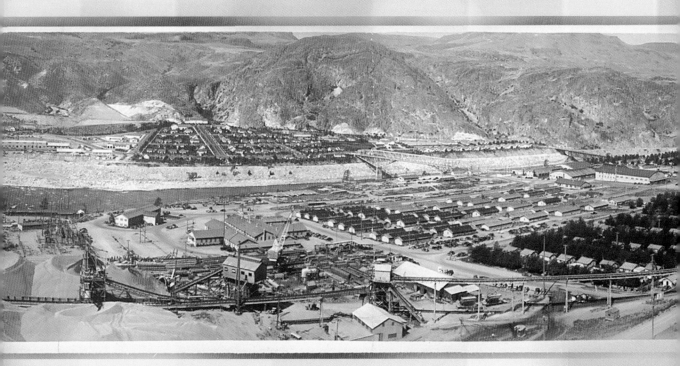

Once World War II started, people in the United States found work in factories making planes, bombs, tanks, and other machines of war. But the labor movement didn't slow down. Guthrie was a true believer in the workers' cause, often playing benefits and other worker events. Even though many of the other folk singers were pacifists, Guthrie was one of the first to admit that the United States needed to fight against the forces of Hitler and Hirohito's Japan. Around this time, he scrawled the words "This Machine Kills Fascists" on his guitar.

*During World War II, Guthrie often performed at **hootenannies**, informal gatherings where everyone could sing and play.*

In 1943, at the young age of 31, Guthrie published his autobiography, *Bound For Glory*. That same year, Guthrie was brought before the **House Un-American Activities Committee (HUAC)**. The Committee's mission was to question Americans suspected of having ties to the Communist Party. The Committee believed that Communists were a threat to the American way of life. Guthrie, who supported many labor unions, was found to have Communist ties. He was **blacklisted** and his music was instantly banned from the radio.

As his family grew, Guthrie recorded less and less, but he never stopped writing. During the years after the war, Guthrie wrote hundreds of lyrics and songs from his house on Mermaid Avenue on Coney Island. Important among these were many children's songs written in a playful, nonsense-rhyming style.

In the late 1940s, tragedy struck Guthrie when a fire broke out in his house, killing his daughter Cathy. The children's songs written for his other kids gave him some measure of comfort. He started to succumb to a degenerative nervous disease called Huntington's Chorea but continued to write songs even as his ability to perform disappeared.

Over the last few years of Guthrie's life when he wasn't in the hospital, he wrote dozens of songs that went unperformed. Woodie Guthrie died in 1967 at the age of 55.

In a sense, folk music came full circle in 1998 when two major artists in the modern folk movement came together to record the works of Woodie Guthrie. Guthrie's daughter Nora approached English folk-rocker Billy Bragg with an interesting proposition: Would he write and record new music to accompany never recorded lyrics written by her father? Bragg accepted the challenge and called upon the band Wilco, whose leader Jeff Tweedy was a huge fan of country and folk. The result of the collaboration between these two folk-based artists was *Mermaid Avenue*, a collection of songs that celebrated the spirit of Woodie Guthrie. The first album became a bestseller and received wide critical acclaim.

Woodie Guthrie's daughter Nora, speaking at a Woodie Guthrie Tribute Concert in Cleveland, OH in 1996.

Pete Seeger and Friends

Guthrie wasn't entirely responsible for the New York City folk music scene. Another important figure in the popularization of folk music was his friend Pete Seeger. Born in New York in 1919, Seeger was from a completely different background. His parents were well-known music educators, artists, and political activists. Although Seeger grew up with music in his house, at first he didn't want to become a musician. Seeger was actually studying to be a sociologist. But the first time he heard the banjo, he quickly changed his mind and started playing. Seeger's interest in music soon led him to seek out Alan Lomax. He traveled with Lomax for a year in 1936, learning the folk songs and ballads of the South.

Pete Seeger (bottom right) with his Almanac Singers, including Woodie Guthrie (top center).

In 1941, Seeger formed the Almanac Singers with his friends and roommates Lee Hays, Woodie Guthrie, and Millard Lampell. The Singers traveled the country playing mostly for audiences of labor organizations that needed some music to cheer them up. The Singers were like a musical pep rally for the union movement. They would win the crowd over with their powerful message and enthusiasm for the music. The lineup of the group changed depending on who was available. Other members included Alan Lomax's sister Bess and singer Burl Ives, as well as Sonny Terry & Brownie McGee. Burl Ives would go on to have a successful career as a folk-pop crossover vocalist. But by the 1960s, Ives was most well known as the voice of the snowman narrator in the animated Christmas special, *Rudolph the Red-nosed Reindeer*.

Burl Ives occasionally sang with the Almanac Singers.

Although they were only around for one year, the Almanac Singers made an impact. They supported progressive causes of the time, like labor rights and civil rights. Although they supported the help that the government had given Americans through the WPA, the Almanac Singers were among the most vocal critics of the United States' participation in World War II. In many ways, their songs were the first of the "protest songs," that would become a hallmark of the folk movement over the years.

The United States' entry into World War II had a dramatic impact on the New York City folk scene. Many of its members were drafted into military service. Song collectors, like Alan Lomax, who worked for the government-run Library of Congress, found that there was no longer funding or materials for recording trips. Fortunately, a folk enthusiast named Moses Asch continued this work, recording artists for his Folkways label.

Pete Seeger was drafted into the army in 1942. While in the army, he performed for troops in the South Pacific conflict, spreading his love of folk music to appreciative audiences. He continued to perform as a traveling solo artist on his return from the war. Eventually, Seeger made his way back to New York City. In 1948 he formed the Weavers with his former Almanac Singers friends Hays Gilbert, Ronnie Gilbert, and Fred Hellerman.

Postwar Folk

The Weavers played pop-influenced versions of songs by Leadbelly, as well as the spiritual ballads of the South.

If the Almanac Singers were rough around the edges, the Weavers were polished. The group had a hit with Leadbelly's "Goodnight, Irene," which topped pop music charts and sold more than 2 million copies. They also had a hit with the traditional song "On Top of Old Smoky." One of the songs the Weavers helped popularize was an African-style chant called "Wimoweh." With its hypnotizing backing vocals *a wimoweh, a wimoweh* and exotic lyric *in the jungle, the mighty jungle, the lion sleeps tonight,* the song was an unlikely smash hit. In 1961, a vocal group called the Tokens recorded a version of "Wimoweh," once again taking it to the top of the pop charts as "The Lion Sleeps Tonight." The success of the song was significant because it marked the beginnings of a more international influence in folk music.

The Weavers' clean, bright vocals and unique style greatly influenced music fans on college campuses across the country. However, in 1955 Seeger, like Guthrie and many of his other contemporaries in music and the arts, was blacklisted by the HUAC. Seeger remained officially blacklisted until 1962. Despite this punishment, Seeger stayed active as an organizer in the folk movement, helping out with many social causes and rallies. He also helped organize the popular Newport Folk Festival, where many folk–blues and country artists from the 1920s and 1930s found an appreciative audience. Seeger also kept writing songs. In 1962, he wrote the song "Turn, Turn, Turn," based on a verse from the Bible. It was eventually recorded by the folk-rock band the Byrds.

Besides John and Alan Lomax, perhaps the most important figure in the recording of folk music was Moses Asch. Throughout the 1940s and beyond Asch made the first commercial recordings of many important folk artists, such as Leadbelly, the Almanac Singers, and Woodie Guthrie. He often recorded musicians whose politics, race, or playing style made them unmarketable to other labels. In the early 1940s, Asch would tape folk artists playing in New York City's coffeehouses and hootenanny circuit. He had no reservations about releasing left-wing or progressive artists.

Besides Seeger and his friends, Asch also recorded bluegrass pioneer Bill Monroe and made field recordings by musicians from every corner of the world. These records were released on labels with names like Asch, Disc, and, most famously, Folkways. In the 1960s, he moved beyond the folk world to make recordings on his Folkways label for the experimental group, the Fugs. Before his death in 1986, Asch made sure his catalog of thousands of unique recordings would be well preserved when he sold them to the Smithsonian Institution. Since 1986, the Smithsonian has made a large number of these recordings commercially available, shining a deserved light on talents long since passed.

Greenwich Village and coffeehouses

The center for the folk scene in New York City from the post-war period through the 1960s was Greenwich Village. Folk music thrived in the many coffeehouses, such as Izzy's Folk Center, and in clubs like the Village Vanguard. Here, artists would try out new material on audiences often made up of other musicians. Not far away was Washington Square Park, where in the 1950s folk musicians strummed guitars in the bright sunshine and lazed about on the grass listening to each other's tunes.

Performers like Ramblin' Jack Elliott kept Woodie Guthrie's songbook alive by performing in coffeehouses, the park, and anywhere else where there was an audience to listen. In the 1950s and 1960s, the Greenwich Village scene would prove a fertile testing ground for rising stars, such as Joan Baez, Bob Dylan, and later, Simon and Garfunkel.

The acoustic guitar was a familiar sight on the streets of Greenwich Village in the 1960s.

Folk Revival

For roughly ten years between the mid-1950s and the Beatles-led British Invasion in 1964, folk music was, for the first time, a bestselling musical genre. This was due to pop-oriented groups, like the Kingston Trio and Peter, Paul & Mary.

One of the first groups to achieve popular mainstream success was the Kingston Trio. They adopted the Weavers' smooth vocal style but dropped the politics. The Trio formed in 1957 around core members Dave Guard, Bob Shane, and Nick Reynolds. Guard learned to play the banjo from studying a "how to" booklet produced by Pete Seeger. The group soon found a local audience at a nightclub called the Purple Onion. They played there weekly for five months in 1957, polishing their sound before embarking on a tour. During the tour, they recorded a ballad called "Tom Dooley" that sold millions of copies. The group went on to record many popular records throughout the 1960s. The Kingston Trio influenced numerous other groups like the Limeliters, the Highwaymen, and the New Christy Minstrels.

The Kingston Trio's happy-go-lucky music and vocal harmonies appealed to non-folk music fans, too.

Mary Travers, Paul Stookey, and Peter Yarrow (right) formed Peter, Paul & Mary in 1961.

One group that took its style from the 1940s New York City folk scene became hugely successful in the 1960s. Peter Paul & Mary became a favorite on the coffeehouse scene in the late 1950s and early 1960s before signing to Warner Brothers Records. Soon after, they scored several pop hits including "Lemon Tree," "If I Had a Hammer," and "Puff the Magic Dragon." But it was the gospel-tinged folk-pop of their cover of Pete Seeger's song "If I Had A Hammer" that would became an anthem of the era's protests and marches everywhere. It was nearly as universal as Seeger's own "We Shall Overcome." Peter, Paul & Mary's music, especially "If I Had a Hammer," was often sung years later at sit-ins and protests against the Vietnam War on college campuses across the country.

The other driving force behind the 1950s folk revival was the release of two collections of folk songs. In 1952, a record collector and filmmaker named Harry Smith released the three-volume collection, *The **Anthology** of American Folk Music*. It featured such blues artists as Blind Lemon Jefferson and Mississippi John Hurt, as well as old recordings of country artists like the Carter Family. *The Anthology* was a collection of music from the 1920s and 1930s, with each volume covering a different type of song—ballads, social music, and songs. The collection caught the attention of a new generation of musicians playing rock 'n' roll and folk music. Music critic Griel Marcus accurately described *The Anthology* as reflective of an "old, weird America" that, by 1952, had long since disappeared.

In 1959, the renowned folklorist Alan Lomax issued the collection *Blues in the Mississippi Night*. This was an album of songs that he had recorded while traveling throughout the South in 1946. It included songs by previously little-known folk-blues artists, such as Big Bill Broonzy and Sonny Boy Williamson. Between Smith's *Anthology* and Lomax's *Blues in the Mississippi Night*, the folk music movement in the United States was again fascinated by the older folk and blues artists.

The Newport Influence

The Newport Folk Festival was the place where many new fans of this old American music first saw original folk-blues and folk artists. Created in 1959, the Rhode Island festival was the gathering place for thousands of fans who had become fascinated by the roots music of the United States. Newport brought together not just traditional folk artists, but also country-blues musicians like Son House, bluegrass legends like Doc Watson, and Cajun musicians. But the lasting impact of the festival was its role as a place where up-and-coming folk singers could start their career with one performance. Joan Baez, Bob Dylan, and Peter, Paul & Mary all got their first big breaks at the Newport Folk Festival.

The Anthology of American Folk Music and the rediscovery of old-time country and blues musicians inspired Pete Seeger's younger brother Mike to form the New Lost City Ramblers. The Ramblers specialized in playing the music of artists from *The Anthology*, such as banjo player Dock Boggs, fiddler Clarence Ashley, and the Carters. They became popular in the Newport folk scene as a sort of living tribute to old music, with instrumentation (fiddle, banjo, guitar) and vocal styles from the 1920s and 1930s.

The Newport Festival was founded by a group of people that included Alan Lomax and Pete Seeger.

NFF

JULY 11 & 12

Mail Order c/o Newport Folk Festival. Newport, R.I. July 11 & 12, 1959. Three performances. Sat. July 11, 8:30 P.M. Sun. July 12, 2:30 P.M. & 8:30 P.M. All seats reserved for evening performances $3, $4 & $5. Sun. afternoon General Admission $2. Include 25¢ for handling with all mail orders.

NEWPORT FOLK FESTIVAL

Featuring the world's largest aggregation of major folk artists-produced by George Wein and Albert B. Grossman
Pete Seeger I Odetta I Kingston Trio I John Jacob Niles I Oscar Brand I Jean Ritchie I Earl Scruggs and The Foggy Mountain Boys I Bob Gibson I Cynthia Gooding I Barbara Dane I The Stanley Brothers I Will Holt I Leon Bibb I Frank Warner I Kossoy Sisters I New Lost City Ramblers I Frank Hamilton I Billy Faier I Sonny Terry and Brownie McGhee I Rev. Gary Davis I Ed McCurdy I Martha Schlamme I New England Folk Dance Society I The Clancy Brothers I Memphis Slim Trio I and workshops and panel discussions

AT NEWPORT, R.I.

Folk singer Joan Baez strumming her acoustic guitar on a beach near her home in California in 1962.

Joan Baez

In 1959, Joan Baez, a beautiful, raven-haired singer with a powerful **soprano** voice, started her career at the Newport Folk Festival. She had only recently started singing while at college, in coffeehouses around Boston. Baez became very popular on the folk scene with that first festival performance. She quickly followed it up with her 1960 self-titled debut album, a collection of her interpretations of traditional folk and blues songs.

For a period in the early 1960s, Joan Baez was a major force in the folk revival, releasing the hit albums *Joan Baez Volume 2* and *Joan Baez in Concert*. She also became known as an early supporter of Bob Dylan, helping spread the word about his songs. Though Baez started as a popular interpreter of traditional songs, she was soon recording political material and taking part in the growing **civil rights** and anti-Vietnam War movements.

Bob Dylan

Dylan's early performances featured traditional ballads and many songs by Woodie Guthrie.

Bob Dylan was a towering figure in folk music in the 1960s. He took folk music beyond its traditional boundaries and widened its appeal to fans of popular music and rock 'n' roll. In just a few short years, he changed folk music forever, plugging it into rock 'n' roll, connecting it with other American roots music like blues and country, and adding a sense of classic poetry.

Born in Duluth, Minnesota in 1941, Dylan started life as Robert Zimmerman. He grew up in the mining town of Hibbing and discovered rock 'n' roll at an early age, starting a rock band in high school. By the time he was in college, Dylan had become a fan of country-folk and blues artists like Leadbelly and Woodie Guthrie, and the romantic work of poets like Arthur Rimbaud and Dylan Thomas. While still in his teens, Bob Dylan decided to become a musician.

When Dylan first arrived in Greenwich Village to make a name for himself, he was simply a Woodie Guthrie cover artist. He wasn't the only one. However, Dylan started writing his own songs and soon got noticed by critics and Columbia Records talent scout John Hammond. Hammond signed Dylan to a recording contract in 1961.

At first, Dylan played folk music in the old tradition. In fact, his self-titled debut record in 1962 featured only two original songs. But by the time he released his follow-up album in 1963, *The Freewheelin' Bob Dylan*, Dylan was writing and performing almost all his own material. Included in this album was Dylan's timeless protest song "Blowin' in the Wind," which became one of the most famous civil rights anthems of the twentieth century.

Dylan drew his style not just from the folk tradition, but also from country-blues and rock 'n' roll. His lyrics were also influenced by European poets. This literary approach resulted in songs that were not obviously political and that didn't just tell stories of the common man. They were personal, **introspective** lyrics that described Dylan's own thoughts. He still wrote powerful political songs, like his 1960s anthem "The Times They Are A-Changin'," but these songs were as much about Dylan as anything else. By the end of 1962, Dylan's massive popularity started the so-called "modern" era of folk where singers wrote about themselves as mirrors of society.

Dylan and Joan Baez on tour in London in 1965.

Over the next few years, Dylan experimented with different styles and wrote hundreds of songs. He also gave some of his many songs to other artists. One such song was "Mr. Tamborine Man," which he gave to the Byrds. Their version of the song is acknowledged as one of the very first folk–rock songs. This makes sense, since Dylan was already starting to move toward more rock-based, electric arrangements. Then in 1965 he released his landmark two-sided single, "Like A Rolling Stone"—a six-minute song that nearly reached the top of the pop charts.

In 1966, Dylan was involved in a serious motorcycle accident that left him laid up for several weeks. Over the following months he recovered indoors and rented a house in Woodstock, New York, that was nicknamed "Big Pink." He spent his time with his Canadian-American backing band the Hawks (who renamed themselves simply, The Band), recording hundreds of songs, ranging from traditional folk songs to simple country numbers and blues jams.

Dylan returned to recording with the 1967 album *John Wesley Harding*, which featured country-influenced songs and simple arrangements. This album was the first country-rock record. His next country-based record, *Nashville Skyline*, was recorded with Nashville session musicians. The record kicks off with Dylan and country legend Johnny Cash performing the duet "Girl From the North Country." Between 1967 and *Nashville Skyline*'s release in 1969, country-rock had become popular, with artists like the Byrds and Gram Parsons scoring hits in the genre.

In 1974, Dylan embarked on an ambitious tour called the Rolling Thunder Revue. The tour featured many of the artists that Dylan had worked with or been influenced by—Joan Baez, Jack Elliott, Guthrie's son Arlo, beat poet Allen Ginsberg, and others.

The Rolling Thunder tour ended up being a sort of review of Dylan's career.

Over the next few years Dylan recorded a half-dozen records and generally kept himself busy. But he was no longer leading rock 'n' roll culture as he had in the 1960s. Starting in 1988, Dylan set out on his Never Ending Tour, playing shows off and on for the next 10 years. Then in 1997 he released an album called *Time Out of Mind* that sold millions of copies and won him another Grammy Award. Dylan hasn't stopped recording and playing live since the late 1980s, and still shows little sign of slowing down. In 2001, he released the award-winning and critically acclaimed album, *Love & Theft.*

Bob Dylan performing in 2004.

Bob Dylan was arguably responsible for moving folk music into a totally different direction. By 1965, the British Invasion and the Beatles had taken the popular music world by storm. Rock 'n' roll had a fresh new face and the folk revival of the early 1960s was rapidly losing its popularity. Rock 'n' roll was loud and amplified. Folk music was usually performed on acoustic instruments and prefered an up-close and personal connection between performer and audience. But artists like Bob Dylan, the Grateful Dead, and the Byrds believed that folk music could evolve by merging with rock 'n' roll.

When Bob Dylan walked out on the stage at the 1965 Newport Folk Festival, he made a clear statement about where he was going. Newport was the most traditional and respected of all the many folk festivals at the time. So, when Dylan plugged in electric guitars and played his folksy hit "Maggie's Farm" at top volume, it was shocking. The crowd booed and, according to legend, Pete Seeger even tried to pull the plug on him. Eventually the set was cut short, but the impact of Dylan "going electric" set the tone for folk's future.

Civil Rights, Folk, and Gospel

Folk music played a major part in providing the soundtrack to the civil rights movement as it developed from the mid-1950s through the mid-1960s. This movement fought for equal rights for African Americans and staged marches and protests throughout the South. Folk music had been political since the 1930s, but in the 1960s protesters and marchers sang a combination of folk music and Southern gospel spirituals to boost their spirits and help form a bond with one another. A good example of this is Pete Seeger's "We Shall Overcome." The tune is based on a gospel hymn, and Seeger's words made it one of the most well-known protest songs.

In 1964, President Lyndon B. Johnson signed the **Civil Rights Act**. But the protests weren't over, and folk music would soon play a role in the anti-war movement against United States' involvement in the Vietnam War.

In August 1963, thousands of people gathered at the Lincoln Memorial in Washington to listen to civil rights' activist Martin Luther King Jr.

The first popular folk singer to discuss the conflict in Vietnam was Phil Ochs. He was called a "singing journalist." His songs were frank stories about the **counterculture** that was protesting the Vietnam War. After his debut album in 1964, *All the News That's Fit to Sing*, Ochs was often compared to Bob Dylan. But Ochs was not as stylistically adventurous as Dylan, and he was more concerned with speaking about social issues than personal ones. *All the News* included the song "Bound For Glory," a title taken from Woodie Guthrie's autobiography. Its attitude was reflective of the changing atmosphere in the United States as a result of the Vietnam conflict and the assassinations of President John F. Kennedy and Martin Luther King Jr.. Ochs' follow-up record, 1965's *I Ain't Marching Anymore*, contained anti-war anthems like "Draft Dodger Rag."

In the mid–1960s, British musicians got in on the folk revival. Young British folk singers weren't just influenced by Dylan and American folk musicians. Bands like Fairport Convention also drew their style from traditional English and Scottish folk music—one of the origins of folk music in the rural United States in the 1800s. Fairport Convention's sound evoked the gentle rolling hills of the English countryside rather than the harsh experience of the Appalachian Mountains in pre-Civil War America. Two of the band's players, Richard Thompson and Sandy Denny, went on to successful solo careers, and the success of Fairport Convention encouraged other folk acts in England.

Fairport Convention took their name from a house called "Fairport" where they rehearsed their music.

Folk Rock

The folk music fans that were shocked by Dylan "going electric" at Newport in 1965 clearly hadn't been paying attention to the developments that started to happen almost immediately after the Beatles' arrival in the United States. In 1965, the Byrds' cover of Dylan's "Mr. Tamborine Man" was the first folk-rock record. The Byrds continued to set trends in popular music by mixing the poetry and vocal harmonizing of Dylan and other folk singers with the rock 'n' roll energy of bands like the Beatles.

Each of the Byrds had emerged from the Los Angeles' folk scene, so they were steeped in the folk tradition. But they were also listening to new music. Roger McGuinn got his start playing acoustic versions of Beatles' songs in Los Angeles coffeehouses as did guitarist and singer David Crosby. Bassist Chris Hillman started out as a **mandolin** player. To the mix they added songwriter Gene Clark's creative imagery accompanied by McGuinn's distinctive guitar sound. This style of playing is characterized by its "chiming" or "jangle" sound, somewhere between the raw power of the electric guitar and the intimate strumming of the acoustic. Ironically, they scored their biggest hit with a version of "Turn, Turn, Turn," written by Pete Seeger, Dylan's stylistic opposite. When Dylan started incorporating country into his mix of folk and rock 'n' roll, so did the Byrds.

Folk-rock bands such as the Byrds became very popular in the 1960s.

Contemporaries of the Byrds, Buffalo Springfield made folk rock that further incorporated country music styles, and spoke frankly about the political atmosphere of the times. The group formed around two main songwriters, Stephen Stills and Neil Young. Though the band only lasted a few years, their 1966 song "For What It's Worth" became a classic:

In 1969, Steve Stills went on to form Crosby, Stills & Nash. The band featured members of Buffalo Springfield (Stills), the Byrds (David Crosby), the Hollies (Graham Nash) and occasionally Stills' former band mate Neil Young. They produced a string of hits that included a cover version of Joni Mitchell's "Woodstock," as well as perhaps their most well-known song, the hopeful "Teach Your Children."

Guitarist Neil Young went on to a successful solo career (both alone and with his backing band Crazy Horse) with albums such as 1972's *Harvest* (with its hit songs "Heart of Gold" and "Old Man"). He also moved into hard rock with records such as 1979's powerful *Rust Never Sleeps*.

Crosby, Stills, Nash, and Young captured the spirit of the early 1970s.

Folk continued to evolve on the non-rock 'n' roll side, too. Folk and folk-rock influenced each other in subtle ways. In 1968, Canadian-born Joni Mitchell released her self-titled debut coproduced by David Crosby of Crosby, Stills & Nash and the Byrds. With Mitchell's unusual voice and poetic lyrics, the album was an immediate success. Her follow-up album, *Clouds*, included the hit and subsequent folk standard, "Both Sides Now."

The pop side of folk-based music, with artists such as James Taylor and Simon and Garfunkel, helped establish the singer-songwriter genre as a soft-edged form of pop rock. FM radio had taken a liking to this style and many of the singer-songwriters had a run of hits in the 1970s. During the early 1970s, soft-rock bands like the Eagles rose to fame on the wave of the popularity of the singer-songwriter genre.

Simon and Garfunkel rose to fame in 1965 with their folk–rock single "The Sound of Silence."

Singer-songwriters like Bruce Springsteen and Kris Kristofferson continued to gain popularity with frank songs about everyday problems that bridge the gap between country, folk, and rock. New Jersey native Bruce Springsteen's 1982 album *Nebraska* was a modern-day rock 'n' roll updating of folk style that owed a debt to Woodie Guthrie.

Bruce Springsteen in concert 1982.

Punk Folk

By the 1970s, folk music had become, frankly, rather dull! It was tame, non-confrontational, and lacked any kind of political message. However, the 1980 election of President Ronald Reagan and British Prime Minister Margaret Thatcher in 1979, combined with the period's tough economic times, spurred a new generation of angry and political folk musicians. These "back-to-basics" performers were inspired by the anger and protest of punk rock music. But they also respected the raw energy and insightful lyrics of Woodie Guthrie and Bob Dylan.

In the United States, artists such as Roger Manning took up this charge. In Britain, the movement was led by London punk musician Billy Bragg. These artists protested against the social and economic conditions of the time with fiery, angry poetry and aggressive acoustic guitar playing.

Their movement was called "anti-folk" or "urban folk." Billy Bragg got his start as a London street musician, playing for occasional tips. He would drag around his beat-up electric guitar and amp and sing in a tone very similar to Woodie Guthrie's stinging criticism of the political Establishment. The style of Bragg and Manning inspired the next generation of folk artists in the 1990s, such as Ani DiFranco.

The British musician Billy Bragg is known for his mix of punk-rock, folk, and protest music.

By the late 1980s, a renewed interest in the old-time music of bands like the Carter Family and early folk-country artists was starting to take hold in the Midwest. It was spearheaded by influential bands like the Belleville, Illinois trio Uncle Tupelo, who mixed their love of punk rock and old-time country in creative new ways. The group so admired early folk music that they recorded an album of 50-year-old country-folk songs and inspired originals called *March 16–20, 1992*. They titled their breakthrough record *No Depression* after a Carter Family song. The music had such an impact that a loosely affiliated group of artists and record labels formed a movement called No Depression (or alternative country).

Uncle Tupelo in 1992. The band broke up in 1994. Jeff Tweedy (left) went on to form Wilco.

Folk's Future

After over a century, recorded folk music continues to change and develop as a new batch of musicians find their own voices. Many of the diverse threads of folk music can now be heard everywhere, from pop radio stations to underground clubs and coffeehouses.

Throughout the 1990s, Ani DiFranco built a growing audience for her punk-political folk style. With the release of her 1995 album *Not A Pretty Girl*, she began to gain more attention for her music outside of her loyal fans. She did this by touring non-stop and writing stirring, emotionally-charged songs. Remarkably, she has managed to resist approaches from the big record labels and releases all her records on her own **independent label**, Righteous Babe Records. An ardent feminest, DiFranco's songs often deal with issues of sexism and inequality that affect women.

Ani DiFranco has been called "a folkie in punk's clothing."

Beck has become one of the most important and creative rock-folk artists of the 1990s and 2000s.

Beck (Beck Hansen) started his career in Los Angeles as a street musician. He became a hit on the Los Angeles club scene with his wild acoustic shows and eventually got the attention of a major label, Geffen Records. His breakthrough album *Mellow Gold* brought a hip-hop feel to folk music and his single "Loser" became an anthem for the generation of twenty-somethings in the early 1990s. Beck became known for his "everything but the kitchen sink" musical style, often blending South American Bossa Nova with rock and hip hop in one song. It's a popular combination, as proved by record sales in the millions of albums like *Odelay* and *Midnite Vultures*. Albums such as *Mutations* and *Sea Change* showcased his simple singer-songwriter side. His 2005 album, *Guero*, was an appropriate mix of Beck's strengths as a rocker and folk songwriter.

Folk-based songwriting continues in new directions, often mixed with grand pop orchestrations, hip hop, and rock 'n' roll. Even after 100 years, American folk music is still alive and breathing.

The new Dylan?

Every once in a while, critics and writers who follow the music scene decide that an artist is "the new Dylan." One such artist is indie rocker Conor Oberst, from Omaha, Nebraska. Oberst was a teenage songwriting **prodigy** and released a series of albums on hometown independent label Saddle Creek. His deeply personal songs, sometimes played with the band Bright Eyes, sometimes solo on acoustic guitar, certainly fit the Dylan mold. Bright Eyes produced some ambitious stylistic experiments, and released two simultaneous albums in 2005—the acoustic-based *I'm Wide Awake, It's Morning* and the techno-influenced *Digital Ash in a Digital Urn*. They became bestsellers, but it is yet to be seen whether Oberst's popularity will last.

Timeline

1861–1865 American Civil War. This war between the Union and the Confederacy ended in 1865 with the defeat of the Confederates.

1865 Thirteenth Amendment to the U.S. Constitution abolishes slavery.

1867 *Slave Songs of the United States* and *The English and Scottish Popular Ballads* sheet music published.

1877 Invention of the phonograph by Thomas Edison.

1885 Huddie "Leadbelly" Ledbetter is born.

1912 Woodie Guthrie is born.

1914–1918 World War I. This war was fought between France, Britain, and the United States against Germany. Germany was defeated in 1918. The United States did not enter the war until 1917.

1920 Commercial radio broadcasting begins in the United States.

1920–1929 The "Roaring Twenties." This decade is also known as the "Jazz Age."

1927 Ralph Peer records the Carter Family and Jimmie Rodgers in Bristol, TN.

1929 The U.S. stock market crash heralds the period of the 1930s known as the Great Depression.

1933 Jimmie Rodgers dies. John and Alan Lomax record Leadbelly.

1935 Leadbelly releases his first record.

1941 The United States enters World War II.

1943 Woodie Guthrie publishes his autobiography *Bound for Glory*.

1945 World War II ends.

1948 Pete Seeger forms the Weavers.

Late 1940s–1973 Period of U.S. involvement in Vietnam.

1952 Harry Smith releases *The Anthology of American Folk Music*.

1959 The first Newport Folk Festival.

Folklorist Alan Lomax releases *Blues in the Mississippi Night*.

1962 Pete Seeger writes the song "Turn, Turn, Turn."

1963 Assassination of President John F. Kennedy on November 22nd

Bob Dylan releases "Blowin' In the Wind."

Martin Luther King Jr. leads a Civil Rights march on Washington, D.C.

1964 Civil Rights Act is signed by President Lyndon B. Johnson.

1965 Bob Dylan plays electric at Newport Folk Festival.

Folk–rock band the Byrds form in Los Angeles, CA.

1967 Woodie Guthrie dies.

1968 Assassination of African-American Civil Rights leader, Martin Luther King Jr. in April.

Assassination of presidential candidate Robert F. Kennedy, brother of late President John F. Kennedy in June.

1969 The Woodstock Festival takes place in Bethel, NY.

1993 Uncle Tupelo release *March 16–20, 1992*.

1998 Billy Bragg and Wilco release *Mermaid Avenue*, a collection of previously unrecorded Woodie Guthrie songs.

Glossary

activism   action taken to achieve political or other goals

acoustic (guitar)   instrument that does not have electric amplification

anthology   collection of works of artists in a single presentation or record

anthropologist   scientist who studies human cultures

ballad   story told in song form, often about a legendary character

blacklisted   to be on a list of people who are being punished for their opinions or actions

Civil Rights Act   set of laws enacted in the United States in 1964 designed to ensure equal protection and rights for African Americans

civil rights (movement)   cultural and political effort to gain equal rights for African Americans in the United States

counterculture   lifestyle of people who reject the dominant values, culture, and behavior of society

cover   when artists record their own, newer version of another artist's music

Dust Bowl (era)   from 1931–1939 in the American southwest-central states (especially Oklahoma), droughts, erosion, and great dust storms caused millions of farmers and others to flee west

epiphany   moment of inspiration

folklorist   someone who studies and documents the folk culture of a place

Great Depression   period from 1929 until the beginning of World War II in which the United States' economy was "depressed," or in poor shape, and many Americans were without work

hootenannies   informal gatherings among members of the folk music scene

House Un-American Activities Committee (HUAC)   from 1938–1975, HUAC interviewed and investigated American citizens in an effort to identify and punish those suspected of "un-American" behavior or Communist sympathy

independent label   record label that is not affiliated with one of the large major labels or another large corporation

introspective   something that looks inward

mandolin   small stringed instrument with a pear-shaped body

multi-faceted   having more than one side or expression

oral tradition   folk method by which songs and stories are passed from generation to generation

pacifist   someone who works to further the cause of peace

prodigy   very young, talented musician

soprano   highest vocal part in a four-part vocal range, or the person who sings within that vocal range

Works Progress Administration (WPA)   one of the so-called "alphabet agencies" of President Franklin Roosevelt's New Deal. It created government-funded jobs during the Great Depression.

yodeling   form of singing in which the singer alternates the sound of their voice from its natural sound to an unnaturally high pitch in rapid succession

Further Information

WEBSITES

Smithsonian Music resources:

www.si.edu/resource/faq/nmah/music.htm

PLACES TO VISIT

MoMI (The Museum of Musical Instruments)

PO Box 8447

Santa Cruz, CA 95061

877-30-MUSIC

www.momi.org

An on-line "museum" with a lot of information on various instruments and genres of music. It includes a large section on Woodie Guthrie.

Experience Music Project

325 5th Ave. N.

Seattle, WA 98109

877-367-5483

www.emplive.org

Huge interactive music museum and archive. Covers all types of popular music—jazz, soul/R&B, rock, country, folk, and blues.

Rock and Roll Hall of Fame Museum

One Key Plaza

751 Erieside Ave.

Cleveland, OH 44114

216-781-ROCK

www.rockhall.com

Huge museum that covers rock, folk, country, R&B, blues, and jazz.

RECORDINGS

The Carter Family:
*Anchored in Love:
Their Complete Victor
Recordings*
(Rounder Records)

Leadbelly:
The Best of Leadbelly
(Cleopatra)

Jimmie Rodgers:
*The Essential Jimmie
Rodgers*
(RCA)

Woodie Guthrie:
*This Land Is Your Land:
The Asch Recordings
Vol 1*
(Smithsonian Folkways)

Pete Seeger:
*Pete Seeger's
Greatest Hits*
(Sony)

Bob Dylan:
Greatest Hits Vol 1
(Sony)

Joan Baez:
Joan Baez
(Vanguard Records)

Bright Eyes:
*I'm Wide Awake, It's
Morning*
(Saddle Creek)

Billy Bragg and Wilco:
Mermaid Avenue Vol. 1
(Electra)

Uncle Tupelo
March 16–20, 1992
(Rockville)

Index